letters to an old friend

poems in the form of letters by:

linda m. crate

Contents

letter 1

dear c. or should i say e?
let's go with e,
if that's what you would prefer.

we were roommates once,
my gran says you were a character;
but i think that's what i liked
most about you that you were so
full of so many different things—

it reminded me of me.

you taught me that my scars
made me beautiful,
and coaxed me out of my shell;

i remember the pink rose you gave me
at the end of our stay as roommates
together—

how you told me i should've told you
about my gallbladder after i got it removed.

i just didn't want to wake you,
and i knew you had finals
like everyone else;

i just didn't want to be a burden—

all my life in certain types of darkness,
i have felt like a burden to those i love;
and i wanted you to soar free as a bird
in the sky without carrying the weight of me.

love,
lili-chan

letter 2

dear e,

there are some days i don't think of you,
but not many.

like that one song from the 80's says:
"there's always something there to remind me"

whether it be the pink bottle
of shaving gel i have in my shower
that reminds me of your little pink car

or a song we listened to together or a
band or musician you introduced me to—

whether it be a character from a book
that reminds me of you,
or one of our shared interests like x-men;

you're spilling out of the pages of my memories
with a soft smile, beckoning me forward—

i remember when you and andy serenaded me
with "linda linda" outside my window,
the only words of that song i could understand;
and it made me laugh so hard—
i don't know if i can laugh that hard again.

love,
linda linda

letter 3

dear e,

i wish i could be courageous,
when i think of courage your face is the one
that shows up in my mind;

i was a bit jealous that you took kira
to model with you once but not me—

i know i am not your traditional model,
but i have a friend in nc and she is plus size
and she models;

i guess i wish you'd have taken a chance
on me—

but i tried not to let it bother me,
she was your friend, too, and you both
had so much fun it made me feel
a little guilty that i was jealous of the experience;

my mother tells me i need to be better
about sharing people—i don't always like to,

even if there's a part of me that knows
that's selfish or not fair;
i just don't want to be forgotten—it's one of my
biggest fears,

sometimes i wonder if you've forgotten me
after all these many moons of silence and distance.
love,
l.

letter 4

dear e,

sometimes i think it would be healthier to let go,
but do we ever really let go of the people
we love?

i don't think so.

they become part of us,
they're woven into the fabric of
our being;

because of you i love peanut butter and bacon sandwiches,
i've seen a purple butterfly, i like pink champagne,
i carry the memories of all those years of friendship we had;

the pictures will never be deleted—
i can't just delete you
by deleting them,
so why bother?

i'm sorry i fell in love with you,
broke the sisterhood;
was too much of a coward to tell you—

something in me broke,
i thought i was going to lose my damn mind;
i thought i was going to go to hell—

was so scared of the look of disgust that i was
certain that would be on your face.

i knew you loved utena,
i'm sorry i couldn't be
your anthy.

love,
not anthy

letter 5

dear e,

i loved that pink rose you
gave me,
to me pink roses
are more
romantic than red;

i searched for a white rose
once,
though,
because that was your favorite;
could only find red—

i apologized,
but you said it was okay;
that red roses were more
fragrant, anyway—

i guess i wonder,
was i a fragrance worth
remembering?

do i still grace the pages
of your memories,
because you're still in mine;

years later.
love,
a thorned rose

letter 6

dear e,

you were like the human equivalent
of sunshine to me;
i remember you said when you were
born there was a supernova

it doesn't surprise me

you were always so full of light
and life and character—

i was a moon,
who appreciated the light
of your sun;

i remember how your fingers
traced over my scar from
my surgery and how you said it
looked like the way some animators
in japan drew flowers—

there are days i feel soft as the
roses you liked to keep,
and others i feel like lestat or alucard
in the darkest most vengeful moments;

i don't know why i'm telling you that—

but if i could apologize and take back
the waves of my ocean that wrecked things,
i would;

believe me, i would.
love,
moon child

letter 7

dear e,

i wonder where you live now,
and if you're happy;

i hope you are—

once i had a dream
in the apartment
that i'm living in now that
we were friends again,

and that you had forgiven me;

i woke up so elated
until i realized it was only
a dream—

then i cried for some time,
i lost track of how long;

some people i don't think you're
meant to lose but sometimes
i have hope that maybe one day
we'll meet again in the future when we're
ready to know each other again—

but if that day never comes,
i am sorry and i should've been honest.

love,
an old friend

letter 8

dear e,

i no longer fear hellfire
or the church;

i realize that romantic love comes in
many different shapes and forms—
so why would it ever be one
boring shape or color?
it wouldn't.

wish i could've accepted
that sooner,

but i was too afraid
of being struck
down by the people i loved
if i were honest with myself
about who i was;

and i remember the conversation
we had about the things
men have done to me and how you
said it's a wonder i even like men still—

i felt my breath catch in my throat
as i said 'yeah' instead of telling you about
my crush on medusa when i was thirteen,
or my crush on lydia deetz or morticia addams;

i just let that conversation fade into ether.
sincerely,
a rainbow hearted girl

letter 9

dear e,

if i ever make it onto the ny times
best seller's list,
will you ever read my book
or books?

will you ever while
away some time
in your living room or the beach
or curled in some corner of
the forest,

reading the words of someone
you once knew?

i don't know if i would rather you did
or didn't for what it's worth;

all i know is that choice isn't mine—

but one day,
if you're listening still;
i hope i can make you proud—
hope that you can look back
on the memories we share
ever so fondly,
and say: "that's my friend."
love,
the dreamer

letter 10

dear e,

i dyed my hair red.
a few times.
i prefer it red, honestly.

i am sorry you never
got to see it,

but maybe you have
through a mutual friend
or something;

i don't know—

sometimes when you pop up
on my memories on facebook
i will go to your profile and look
at your latest photos;

just to know you are okay
and to torture myself

because a part of me feels like
i deserve to feel hurt
for hurting you—

i am sorry.
i miss you.
love,
regret

letter 11

dear e,

i remember how i said
the ewoks reminded me of
teddy bears and you said "no!"
but they were so cute and i wanted
to give them all hugs;

a lot of my life i have felt like an
outsider,
sometimes even a stranger in my bones;

but you always made me feel welcome,
always made me feel like i belonged—

always let me nerd out,
speaking of nerdy things i play this game
now which has this race called lumé;
and the female variant of it reminds me of you—

speaking of variants,
have you watched loki?
it highly disappointed me,

but i'm hoping new seasons will be better;
and i am hoping that we will see thor
in both the movies and this show reunited—

guess time will tell,
but i thought there would be a lot more
female variants and i'm a bit upset
there was only one because i don't really
like sylvie.
love, linda

letter 12

i remember visiting
you in erie,

meeting your friend
cody and hanging out with
him and josh;

i remember going to that one
bar we went to before going
to the gay bar where i got an
appletini and it was the best one
i ever had—

but i can't remember the name of
the bar, honestly;

all i remember of the gay bar
is how we sat at the tables
mostly drinking our drinks—

it was that visit that you showed me
repo! the genetic opera,
and i fell in love
with it;

except for the ending because i felt bad
for mag.
love,
sympathy for the blind

letter 13

dear e,
once i was a flower girl
at my mother's wedding
throwing pink rose petals,

if i could go back in time
then i'd grab you a rose
which wasn't used for my basket;

but even if time isn't linear
it doesn't allow me
to go back and be the person
i should've always been—

so i'm becoming me,
as you're becoming you;

oceans between us washing away
the sands of our youth and there's
me that wonders if one day

we might thread together new memories
among the stars and discover more purple butterflies.
love,
the flower girl

letter 14

dear e,

i remember that one time
we went to dracula's ball,

and i had a blast;

for the most part
aside from that lady
with her whip in a situation
i didn't ask to be a part of—

and i vowed to myself that
one day i would go again,

it was a lot of fun;

and i wonder if i did go
if we might both be in the same
room

unaware of each other—

two souls once tethered
now parted,
i wonder if we'd sense one another.
love,
dracula's daughter

letter 15

dear e,

i have written scads
of poems about you
through the years and i wonder
if you've read any of them;

or if any of them have touched your soul—

but maybe you don't read poetry
so it's easier to avoid my words,

i don't blame you if that's the case;

sometimes i refer to you as a fae
and myself as the vampire because it
seems fitting that you're the beautiful one,
and i am the one that's cursed;

sometimes you are the coyote and i am the
raven two creatures misunderstood in our own
different ways—

i wish i could find a way to undo all the
hurt that i caused but i can't sew the past in different threads.
sincerely,
a girl who used to sew

letter 16

dear e,

i am sorry
for the misunderstanding
we had,
and my assumptions
that broke apart our friendship;

i wish that i could take back
the hurt i caused you—

i tend to push away
before i can be rejected,
and yet now i can see
your intention wasn't what
i assumed;

you were trying to protect yourself
i was, too—

but i didn't mean for your heart
to get caught in the crossfire
of my temper,

i didn't mean to destroy
every temple of our friendship;

until only moons, suns, and
oceans could be the measure of
all the time that stood between us.
sincerely,
the vampire

letter 17

dear e,

have you seen the barbie
movie yet?
i haven't.

when i was little
i despised the color pink,

but then i met you;

and it didn't seem to be
such an awful color
any longer—

i see you in pink cars,
girls with pink hair,
and in pink sunsets that fall
into my window offering
me warmth that feels like your love;

and it makes me both smile and sad
that all these years later you're
still with me

even when we're miles apart—

you're living your life,
and i am living mine;

wondering if one day our paths
may intersect or if that's even
what either of us may want or need?

it's so hard to say,
something our hearts want
may exactly undo us because
they are wild things with wings only
recognizing the music of things.
love,
the poet

letter 18

dear e,

sometimes my mother still
asks about you,
maybe she misses the
happiness our friendship gave me;

i don't know—

and i try not to let it bother me,
but the loss of you shattered
a part of me;

i don't know if i can get that
part of me back

so i press on without it—

i see the moon and sometimes i
wonder if you look at the moon
sometimes and think of me,
the way i look at her in all of her
phases and see beauty
reminds me of the way you used
to look at me;

you were always a sun that brightened
up the darkest days of my sky—

you woke up the dreaming
in me when i thought
she was dead and gone,
and shook me out of the numb dread
of where i pressed on simply in aching;

you reminded me magic still existed.
love,
the witch

letter 19

dear e,

i remember when my
dad first met you
he thought you were
a hippy,

i wasn't sure what i thought
but i knew somehow you
were different from everyone else
i had ever known;

and i was right—

years after we stopped talking
i met a boy that reminded me of you,

he was canadian and loved the maple leaves, too;

i fell so fast, too fast;
and as you can imagine he broke
my heart and my wings just because he could—

it took me a while to remember
my magic, after that,

but i am standing taller and brighter than when i met him;

and i wonder if he wasn't my karma
for hurting you—
& if you ached as badly as he made me hurt,
then i know no simply apology would suffice;

i'd give you a garden of white roses if i could.
love,
hindsight is 20/20

letter 20

dear e,
i saw a video of laurell k. hamilton
talking about jean claude this
morning,
and i thought of you;

i remember when we were
roommates you had that poster
of him hanging on the wall

and i couldn't stop admiring his abs—

vampires have always been
my favorite monster,

i may have never met my father
but i have often imagined
him as a vampire;

sometimes he stays away from me
to protect me

sometimes he wants me to stay with him

& other times he tries to kill me—

i don't know what to say except i am sorry
even if it is never enough to make up for

what i did, even if i must live the rest of my
life without you.
love,
the vampire's daughter

letter 21

dear e,

i remember i read
the entirety
of the first lord of the rings
book when i visited you
in philly;

had never been able to push
through it before without your
encouragement because
while i loved the hobbit this book was
more dense with descriptions of
trees that made me flip through the pages to
see when said description might end—

i found a character that wasn't in
the movies that i fell in love
with immediately: tom,

and i asked you if he was in any of the
other books and you said not really
and it made me quite sad;

it is like me to fall in love with the weird
side-character because i've felt like that
most of my life—

i wanted to be xena when i played
with my friend,
but she never let me because she
was the one with dark hair like xena;
and i was the one that looked like
gabrielle—

i just wanted my main character moment
for once in my life,
but even in play my friend wouldn't allow for that.
love,
gabrielle

letter 22

dear e,

becoming is hard,
yet i think it is also
rewarding;

hard to wash away
all the branding of
your youth and step into
who you are meant to be

in a world that doesn't
appreciate those who are
different—

but people like you & i weren't
meant to fit in, but stand out;

i think you learned and embraced
that fact long before i was
able to—

but i am coming into who i was
always meant to be,
wish you could see that i am doing
better than when you knew me;

i hope you are happy where you are.
sincerely,
a better me

letter 23

dear e,

i remember when you dyed
the tips of my hair pink,
and the top of my hair purple
but that ended out just washing
out to pink;

my mother said she was fine with it
but i could tell by her expression
she hated it—

i remember watching star trek
with you because it was easier than
facing the silence that existed
between me and m.

i tried so hard to love him in a way
that he needed,

but i just couldn't be dragged down by
the depression he faced any longer;
it was just too heavy and haunting—

and i am sorry if i made you feel awkward,
i know that sometimes i gave you this
look that screamed "help" because i didn't
know what else to do;

but you always tried to help me and i appreciate that.
love,
the haunted

letter 24

dear e,

i remember you were excited
when i got with a,
but honestly no one warned me
about how they were bipolar;

paradise was quickly lost—

but i remember when they broke
up with me,
you told me that i shouldn't get
sad but allow myself to get angry

maybe anger is better at
burning bridges we don't need

to stand on than sadness—

i have always been a good swimmer,
after all,
i thought it was funny when you said
that i looked like a mermaid with a land boy
in my one photo with m. because that
was always my nickname when i was younger;

if there was a body of water that's where
i wanted to be—

apparently when i was one,
they took me to a lake,
and i tried running to the water before
someone picked me up.
love,
the mermaid

letter 25

dear e,

i wonder if you ever watched
the secret garden when you
were growing up because that was
one of my favorite movies,

i've grown out of liking anything potter
related because of rowling and her
views on my trans and non-binary friends;

still love lord of the rings, though,
because it still stands the test of time all
these years later—

i remember when you once told me
your wedding dress would be green,
and it just reminded me of every
lush and wonderful forest i have ever walked;

every slant of magical light dancing through
the leaves is the exact shades of green
i imagined you might wear—

saw a galaxy wedding dress in black and gold,
and i think if i were to ever be married
i might wear something like that because while i
love the trees and the seas and the creeks
i have always known, i have always been obsessed

with the idea of walking among the clouds.
love,
cloud walker

letter 26

dear e,

my maternal grandmother's mother
had the maiden surname starr,
so i know that i was born
to shine;

maybe not as bright as the sun
of your core

but as the moon that i have
always
known myself to be—

you gave me such music and melody
when you were a part of my life,
thank you for the lessons and for all
of the adventures and love;

i wish that it was still happening but i know
we're both different people now—

maybe in the next life
we will know each other better,
maybe then i won't break your heart;
and maybe in that one you could
love me back—

see me as more than a sister.
love,
a starr

letter 27

dear e,

i remember you telling
me about the pirates
that used to navigate the
waters

as we drew closer to
philly,

and i remember looking out
to see all of those rocks trying to imagine
how tall the water may have been
then;

i remember going to visit your sister
at college and seeing how massive

the gray squirrels were—

none of the ones around here have
ever been that big from what
i've seen,

although some of them pose
for pictures and it makes me wonder
if they weren't models or actors in
one of their past lives.
love,
a not so pirate's life for me

letter 28

dear e,

you may have been
the pink-haired revolutionary
utena,

but i was usagi
who could create worlds
out of nothing and bring back
people from the dead;

yet i couldn't resurrect our friendship
from the dead no matter how many
times i tried—

artemis and luna have left,
there is no diana here, either;

i feel truly alone—

even wild roses scream to me
of your name,
every pink sunset fills me with both
joy and regret;

i wonder if i picked up a sword
would i become a new moon

one worth knowing?

i don't think i have anything to lose.
love,
usagi

letter 29

dear e,

my best friend now
loves white roses,
too;

and i cannot help but
smile—

the universe always has
some way to remind me of you,
even when i just let things
flow and don't even try there's always
something whispering your name;

maybe this is my penance
for hurting you—

i'm sorry that i wasn't brave enough
to tell you how i felt,
but i didn't know how to accept how
i felt let alone tell you;
and i was certain that you would
reject our friendship as well as my love
should i have been honest—

yet burying that truth inside
didn't kill it,

the flower blooms every day
reminding me all these years later
that you have and always will exist

in my memories.
love,
the grave digger

letter 30

dear e,

i got my driver's license,
have to renew mine soon;

tried to just order one
with my old picture
but they want me to come
into the dmv—

they still don't care if they
inconvenience people

without cars,

but i'm not surprised;
people don't seem to mind
wasting your time

that's why i prefer to be in
nature and in solitude—

i have found healing
in the trees, in the breeze,
and in the songs of sun and moon;

i have found nature accepts
me wilds and all—

when i walk the trees,
sometimes i wonder if the same sun
has kissed us both that day;

i wonder if we ever drank in the
same wild air.
love,
the hermit

letter 31

dear e,

i remember going to
the ren faire together,
you told me to watch out
for the sangria punch;

but it was so good
that i couldn't resist—

came across a picture
of leotie from that day,

i don't remember much about
that day other than the hat
you liked on me and the photo
of you and leotie in that coffin;

i just remember that it was a good day—

wish there were more of them to share,
but sometimes good things come to an end;
and we must move on even when we'd
rather crawl into their bones and sip on the
sweet nectar years later.
love,
reminiscing hummingbird

letter 32

dear e,

i remember our walk
at edinboro one autumn around
the lake,

autumn has always been my
favorite of seasons;

dressed up in her many colors—

like anne of green gables
i'm grateful we live in a world with
octobers,

and i am grateful to live in a world where
i got to know you;

because i've never felt like anyone's
favorite person and yet i never felt like
your second choice—

i felt like we belonged in each other's lives,
and i find that you're unforgettable as
the song by ani difranco and jackie chan;

and if i had some hindsight in the past
i would've thrown two shoes in the lake

so like kate bush i could walk upon
the waters of my past and feel them
in my present.
love,
undone by music

letter 33

dear e,

thank you for waking the
dreams and the magic
in me when i thought they
were dead and gone in me;

i'll forever be in your debt
for that—

because this phoenix
forgot her fires,
and how to rise from the ashes
prior to meeting you;

and i have risen many times
since—

every time a pink sunset falls upon
my skin,
i wonder if it isn't you saying hello
or perhaps goodbye;

but i have always hated goodbyes because
they feel final whereas a hello

opens the door again to perhaps a new adventure—

i'd welcome new adventures with you,
but they probably wouldn't be the same
as they once were.
love,
the nostalgic one

letter 34

dear e,

i have a tendency to dwell on things
a bit too long,
if you haven't noticed;

they say it's better to let go instead
of hurting yourself but i have always

struggled with goodbyes—

i let the past haunt me longer than i should,
but those i love have never truly left me
even when they've walked away
years ago;

i am the girl that remembers every love
as well as every scar,
maybe that's why i am always bleeding
blood that isn't mine—

slipping in the memories of the past,
i tell myself i should just let you go;

but once i love—i will forever love
unless you deliberately harm me or my heart,
and you did neither of those things;

i am sorry that i let my fear drive a wedge
between us—

wish i had been strong enough to simply work
through my problems on my own,
without taking anything out on you.
love,
incapable of saying goodbye

letter 35

dear e,

you may ask me,
what is the point of all these letters?
what is the point of cutting yourself
open and bleeding on all of these pages?

i am digging up bones of the past
that could hurt me,
so why don't i just put the shovel down?

i think i just needed to tell you about
everything even if you may never
read these words,

to give me some sort of catharsis from
the grief of all the things i never got a chance to say;

i've published many books of poetry now
and even some of my prose
yet without you by my side sometimes
it feels like an empty promise

or a hollow prayer—

i have gone on with my life existing,
but i want to live again;

maybe one day i will find a cure
to all this melancholy inside me and i will find
the music and magic i have been missing
since you walked away.
love,
the hopeful

letter 36

dear e,

don't feel bad for me,
you did what you could;
and i should've shown you
more gratitude and less
anger—

i wish i hadn't pushed you
away out of my fear,
i wish i hadn't made a mistake
out of fear,
wish i hadn't said hurtful things
out of fear;

no one wants to live their life
in fear and i should've never
let it lead me to the place where
it ended our friendship—

when i realized what i felt for you,
i spent years looking out stained glass
windows and looking at the cross and
praying not to be queer but the creators
of the universe never took that part
away from me;

so maybe i should've prayed for
acceptance, for compassion, for mercy
instead—

perhaps, i always knew the song of the church
was never for me.
love,
the worrywart

letter 37

dear e,

sometimes left alone
with my thoughts
is dangerous,

they can veer into
unchartered territory;

sometimes my imagination
can be a beautiful place
where i enjoy tranquility

but paired with my anxiety
sometimes it becomes
a wasteland full of dark thoughts—

i don't know if we'll ever know
each other again in this life,

a part of me is hopeful we will;
another says that knowing you once
was gift enough and another part
thinks perhaps the universe parted us to
protect us both from the ugliest parts
of ourselves—

but i want to believe in never never land,
and fly away with peter pan; and find a universe
for you and i.
love,
faith, trust, and pixie dust

letter 38

dear e,

i'm not always patient,
i talked to a a woman who
read fortunes;

she told me to wait until
august one year to contact you

i reached out sooner and there
was no response and i was so
ashamed that i didn't bother
trying to reach out again—

don't know why i couldn't just wait,
but waiting has always been the hardest
part for me;

feels like most of my life i have been
waiting for some moment i cannot describe—

i wanted to jump into the water like i
did when i danced in the creek
one summer with the
crows,

but sometimes good things take time;
and maybe i should've just ought've enjoyed
the music in the meantime.
love,
the impatient one

letter 39

dear e,

i remember when you said
you wanted to go to this
underground club with me,

but decided against it because
we were going to dracula's ball the
next weekend;

i wouldn't have minded going
to two different places

i have always craved experiences
and my curious nature would've probably
led me to enjoy both—

instead we had starbucks and explored
the mall,

sometimes they have good sales
at that mall;
but i don't remember if they did that
day or not—

i only remember my cupcake was too sweet
and i have always had a sweet tooth so i was taken
by surprise.
love,
the sweet tooth

letter 40

dear e,

i guess this is goodbye for now,
as i've started to run out of things to say
that i haven't said before;

i hope that you're becoming who you've
always wanted to be and discovering
bits and bobs of yourself
to sew together

into the fabric of your being—

i remember being a part of the production
you had a part of leading:
"bang, bang you're dead" sometimes
that's what it feels like the title of the romance
section of my life should be titled
but i digress,

thank you for being a part of my life;
the good, the bad, and everything between
helped shape me into becoming a better person—

& i know there is enough magic in this
world to revive everything in my heart that is broken

so i am going to trust in it now—

& maybe one day we will get to know one another again,
but if we shouldn't—i will be okay, and i know you will be okay;
maybe next life we can be better suited to know another.
love,
she who trusts magic

9 789356 672758